Kebabs &

Sangeeta Khanna

A Sterling Paperback

STERLING PAPERBACKS
An imprint of
Sterling Publishers (P) Ltd.
A-59, Okhla Industrial Area, Phase-II, New Delhi-110020
Ph. : 26387070, 26386209, Fax : 91-11-26383788
E-mail: ghai@nde.vsnl.net.in

Kebabs & Snacks
©2003, Sterling Publishers (P) Ltd.
ISBN 81 207 2550 6

All rights are reserved. No part of this publication may be reproduced, stored in a retrieval system or transmitted, in any form or by any means, mechanical, photocopying, recording or otherwise, without prior written permission of the publisher.

Published by Sterling Publishers Pvt. Ltd., New Delhi-110020.
Lasertypeset by Vikas Compographics, New Delhi-110020.
Printed at Sai Early Learners Press (P) Ltd.

Weights and Measures

The weights and measures used in this book are in grams and standard weighing cups. One cup measures approximately 200 gm and 1 level teaspoon is equivalent to approximately 5 gm. Similarly, 1 level tablespoon is equivalent to approximately 15 gm or 3 teaspoons.

The oven temperature for baked dishes is usually 200°C, which is equivalent to approximately 400°F or gas mark 6.

About the book

This book brings to you a wide array of delectable snacks with easy-to-follow recipes. They are ideal to whip up in a jiffy for unexpected guests, perenially hungry children or just for those in-between times. They are made from ingredients which are readily available. All the servings in this book are for four to six persons.

A glossary has also been provided for the guidance of the reader. The accompanying colourful illustrations are a visual feast.

The carefully selected recipes are sure to tantalise every palate.

Contents

Glossary	6
Bread Treats	10
Rolls, Kebabs and Cutlets	34
Pakoras, Balls and Kachoris	55
Others	79

Glossary

Ajinomoto	: *Chinese salt, known as monosodium glutamate*
Bengal gram	: *Chane ki dal*
Black pepper	: *Kali mirch*
Black salt	: *Kala namak*
Brown sugar	: *Shakkar*
Capsicum	: *Shimla mirch*
Caraway seeds	: *Shah jeera*
Cardamom	: *Elaichi*
Cashewnuts	: *Kaju*
Celery	: *An aromatic herb*
Chickpeas	: *Chana*
Coconut	: *Nariyal*
Coriander	: *Dhaniya*
Corn	: *Makki*
Cornflour	: *Makki ka atta*
Cottage cheese	: *Paneer*

Cumin	: Jeera	Mint	: Pudina
Curry powder or Kitchen King masala	: A blend of salt, cumin powder, cinnamon, nutmeg powder, cardamom, peppercorns and artificial flavourings	Molasses sugar	: Treacle or sugar syrup
		Mustard	: Rai
		Pomegranate seeds	: Anardana
		Raisins	: Kishmish
		Screwpine	: Kewra
		Semolina	: Suji
Dry mango powder	: Amchoor	Sesame	: Til
Flour	: Maida	Spinach	: Palak
Garam masala	: Whole spice powder	Thymol	: Ajwain
		Turmeric	: Haldi
Garlic	: Lasun	Vermicelli	: Sevai
Ginger	: Adrak	Vinegar	: Sirka
Gram flour	: Besan	Walnuts	: Akhrot
Margarine	: Unsaturated fat		

White sauce: 1 tbsp butter, 1 tbsp flour, 1 or 1½ cups milk, ½ tsp each of salt and pepper. Melt the butter in a pan and add the flour. Stir for a minute on a low flame. Add the milk, stirring continuously. Then add salt and pepper. Cook till it starts to coat the spoon. Take it off the fire and use as required.

Breadcrumbs: To make a cup of breadcrumbs, take 3 slices of dried or toasted bread. Break them into pieces and then grind in a grinder.

For Italino sauce: 5 tomatoes, blanched and pureed, ½ cup chopped onions, 1 tsp oregano, 1 tsp crushed garlic, 2 tsp red wine (optional), 2 tbsp olive oil, salt and pepper to taste

Pour the olive oil into a pan, add the onions and garlic and saute for 2 minutes. Add the pureed tomatoes and let it simmer on a medium flame for 5 minutes. Stir occasionally. Add all the other ingredients and bring to the boil. Keep aside.

Vegetable Parcels (pg.112) →

BREAD TREATS

Bread Fingers

Ingredients

½ cup cottage cheese, crumbled
½ cup grated cheese
½ cup each of grated carrot and cucumber
1 tsp ground green chillies
2 grated onions
¼ cup chopped coriander leaves
1 loaf of sliced bread, with crust removed
2 tbsp butter
Salt to taste

Method

1. Squeeze out the water from the carrot, cucumber and onion and mix well. Add the cottage cheese to it.
2. Mix the green chillies, coriander leaves, butter and salt. Make into a paste.
3. Mix this paste with the carrot-cucumber-onion mixture.
4. Cut the bread slices diagonally and apply the paste on them. Sprinkle the grated cheese on them.
5. Bake at 200°C for 10 minutes.
6. Serve hot.

5. Put the bread slices in salted water and remove immediately. Squeeze out the water.
6. Place the cottage cheese filling on one half of the slice, and fold the other half over to cover it. Press down the edges to shape it like a patty.
7. Heat the oil. Roll the patties in the breadcrumbs and fry in the hot oil.
8. Serve hot with tomato sauce.

Cheese Delight with Paneer Crumbs

Ingredients

½ cup cottage cheese, coarsely mashed
50 gm processed cheese
½ green chilli, finely chopped
1" piece ginger, grated
1 cup chopped coriander leaves
25 gm butter
4 tbsp milk
12 slices of bread, with crusts removed
¼ tsp chilli powder
¼ tsp salt
Oil for frying

Method

1. Slice the loaf, but do not slice through, leaving a 2 cm base undisturbed.
2. Mix the butter with the garlic paste, salt and pepper.
3. Butter the slices on both sides with the paste.
4. Place the loaf on a foil and spread the rest of the butter on it. Wrap the foil and bake for 10 minutes.
5. Open the foil on top and bake for another 5 minutes.
6. Serve hot covered in foil.

Garlic Bread (pg.17) →

Russian Sandwiches

Ingredients

8 tsp butter
1 tsp red chilli sauce
1 or 1½ tsp tomato ketchup
½ cup processed cheese, grated
½ tsp salt
½ tsp mustard powder
1 loaf of bread

Method

1. Mix the butter, tomato ketchup, salt, chilli sauce and mustard powder into a soft paste.
2. Cut the bread lengthwise in ½ cm thick slices. Remove the hard crusts.
3. Spread the soft paste with a flat knife and then the grated cheese.
4. Roll up each slice, wrap each roll in butter-paper, fix it with toothpicks and chill.
5. Cut the rolls into ½ cm thick slices before serving.

Sandwich Cake

Ingredients

1 loaf of bread, cut lengthwise into 3 strips
A few lettuce leaves and French fries
1 cup white sauce

For the filling

1 cup mashed cottage cheese
½ cup each of potatoes and carrots, boiled and chopped
½ cup finely chopped capsicum
Salt and pepper to taste

For the topping

1 cup green peas, ground into a fine paste
1 tbsp lime juice
2 tbsp butter
Salt and pepper to taste

Method

1. Combine all the ingredients for the topping.
2. Add half of the white sauce to it. Mix well.
3. Mix the ingredients for the filling.
4. Add the remaining white sauce to it and mix well.

For assembling

1. Apply the butter on one side of the bread and arrange it on a tray covered with the lettuce leaves.
2. Spread half of the filling on it.
3. Take another slice and butter it on both sides. Place over the filling.
4. Spread a second layer of the filling. Butter the third slice on one side and place with the buttered side down on the second filling.
5. Cover the top slice of the bread with the topping mixture. Level it with a knife and decorate with thin strips of French fries.
6. Chill, cut into thick slices and serve.

Stuffed Loaf

Ingredients

1 cup crumbled cottage cheese
1 loaf of bread
1 onion, finely sliced
½ cup finely chopped capsicum
1 tomato, finely chopped
2 tbsp each of chopped coriander leaves and tomato sauce
4 tbsp butter, ¾ tsp salt
1/3 cup breadcrumbs
1 tbsp each of finely chopped green chillies
and grated processed cheese
¼ tsp Worcestershire sauce
Pepper and chilli powder to taste

Method

1. Cut the bread slices into round shapes. Apply the butter on both sides and keep aside.
2. Heat 2 tablespoons of butter. Add the onion to it and saute for 2 minutes.
3. Add the green chillies, coriander leaves, cottage cheese, chilli powder, tomato, salt, pepper and chilli powder. Cook for 2 more minutes, then add the capsicum.
4. Add the breadcrumbs, tomato sauce and Worcestershire sauce and keep aside to cool.
5. Then spread the filling on one round bread slice and cover it with another. Sprinkle the cheese on it and place on a greased tray. Bake at 200°C for 10 minutes and serve hot.

Sesame Toasts

Ingredients

4 slices of bread (with edges trimmed)
2 tbsp sesame seeds, Oil for deep frying

For the topping

2 tbsp oil
1 tsp each of ginger paste, garlic paste, ajinomoto and soya sauce
1 cup finely chopped mixed vegetables (spring onions, cabbage, carrots and mushrooms)
¼ cup blanched and mashed tomato
¼ tsp each of black pepper and chilli powder
Salt to taste

For the paste

3 tbsp flour, A little water to make a thick paste

Method

1. Add a little water to the flour and make a thick paste. Keep aside.
2. Heat 2 tablespoons of oil in a pan, add the ginger and garlic pastes and fry lightly for a few seconds. Add the vegetables and ajinomoto. Stir-fry over a high flame for a minute.
3. Add the remaining ingredients for the topping and stir-fry for another minute. Remove from the pan and cool to room temperature. Divide it into 4 portions.
4. Take a slice of bread, spread the vegetable mixture and level it well. Then spread a little flour paste on top and sprinkle the sesame seeds all over it. Prepare the remaining slices of bread in the same manner.
5. Heat the oil in a frying pan. Deep-fry the bread with the coated side down. Then turn over and fry the other side. Both the sides should be golden brown. Cut each piece into a triangle as shown in the picture.

Sesame Toasts (pg.27) →

Vegetarian Burger

Ingredients

¼ cup crumbled cottage cheese
6 plain burger buns
1 onion, finely chopped
½ cup boiled noodles
¼ cup each of boiled corn kernels and finely chopped carrots
25 gm processed cheese
2 tbsp oil
1 tbsp each of tomato sauce and soya sauce
1 tsp each of chilli sauce and vinegar
A pinch of sugar
Salt to taste

Method

1. Scoop out the buns. Crumble the scooped portion of buns and keep aside.
2. Pour the oil into a frying pan. Fry the onion, cottage cheese, noodles, corn kernels and chopped carrots with the sauces added to them. Add a pinch of sugar and fry for 5 minutes. Then add salt, ajinomoto and white sauce.
3. Mix some crumbs of the bun to the vegetables.
4. Refill the buns with the filling. Sprinkle the grated cheese as a topping and bake for 10 minutes at 200°C. Serve hot.

Corn Delight

Ingredients

½ cup boiled or tinned corn kernels
1 tomato, cut into wedges
½ cup crumbled cottage cheese
1 tbsp each of lime juice, cream and butter
2 tbsp eggless mayonnaise (readymade)
1 tsp each of garlic paste and onion paste
1 tbsp finely chopped spring onions
8 slices bread
½ tsp pepper powder
Salt to taste

Method

1. Mix all the ingredients except the bread. Keep aside. Cut the bread into squares.
2. Spread the mixture on the bread squares.
3. Grill them till they are golden brown.
4. Serve hot, garnished with tomato wedges on the side.

ROLLS, KEBABS AND CUTLETS

Creamy Paneer Cubes

Ingredients

½ cup flour, 1 tbsp lime juice
2 tbsp each of tomato sauce and grated cheese
1 tsp each of cumin seed powder and chilli powder
1 tsp green chilli paste
A little milk or water to make batter
A pinch of baking powder
100 gm cottage cheese, cubed
Semolina for coating
Oil for deep frying
Salt to taste

Method

1. Make a thick batter of the flour, cheese, tomato sauce, green chilli paste and salt. Add the milk and baking powder and beat with a beater.
2. Pour the lime juice in a bowl along with a tablespoon of water, salt, chilli and cumin seed powders. Coat the cottage cheese pieces in it and keep aside for 10 minutes.
3. Then dip the cottage cheese pieces in the batter, roll in the semolina and deep fry.
4. Serve with a toothpick inserted into each cottage cheese cube.

Mushroom Paneer Kebab

Ingredients

200 gm mushrooms
200 gm cottage cheese
2 tbsp thick curd (water drained)
1 tsp garam masala
1 tsp each of ginger and garlic paste
½ tsp freshly ground pepper
1 tbsp lime juice
1 tbsp butter
Salt to taste

Method

1. Remove the stems of the mushrooms. Keep aside.
2. Cut the cottage cheese into the size of ice-cubes and keep aside.
3. Mix the rest of the ingredients except the butter. Marinate the mushrooms and cottage cheese cubes in this mixture. Keep aside for 2 hours.
4. Thread the mushrooms and cheese cubes onto a skewer alternately.
5. Grill over a hot charcoal fire for 5 to 10 minutes till the mushrooms are grilled.
6. Keep brushing them with the butter from time to time for a crisper taste.
7. Serve hot.

Palak Paneer Kebab

Ingredients

½ cup spinach paste
2 tbsp mint chutney
2 tbsp curd
1 tbsp butter
½ tsp chat masala
½ tsp black salt
200 gm cottage cheese
½ tsp ginger-garlic paste

Method

1. Cut the cottage cheese into thick slices and keep aside.
2. Mix the rest of the ingredients and make a paste.
3. Apply this paste on the cottage cheese slice and keep aside for 4 to 5 hours.
4. Arrange the pieces on a greased baking dish and bake at 250°C for about 10 minutes.
5. Serve hot.

Paneer Kebab

Ingredients

200 gm cottage cheese
1 onion, finely chopped
1 capsicum, finely chopped
1 tbsp butter
1 tsp tandoori colour
3 tbsp white sauce
3 tbsp corn kernels, tinned or fresh
½ tsp chat masala
¼ tsp black salt
Salt and pepper to taste

Method

1. Make a slab of the cheese, about 6" by 6" in size. Coat it with the *tandoori* colour and keep aside.
2. Melt the butter. Fry the onion, capsicum and corn kernels in it. Add the white sauce to it, along with all the *masalas*.
3. Spread this topping on the cottage cheese. Bake at 200°C for 5 to 10 minutes.
4. Cut into desired shapes and serve.

Paneer Vermicelli Rolls

Ingredients

200 gm grated cottage cheese
250 gm potatoes
½ cup grated onion
1 cup vermicelli, 2 slices bread
½ tsp each of ginger and garlic paste
1 tsp green chilli paste
½ tsp sugar, 1 tsp chilli powder
1 tbsp chopped coriander leaves
Juice of ½ lime
Oil for deep frying
Salt to taste

Method

1. Boil the potatoes, peel and mash them.
2. Add the ginger, garlic and green chilli pastes.
3. Then add the coriander leaves and lime juice to it and mix well.
4. Remove the crust from the bread slices and soak in water. Squeeze out the water and mash well. Add to the potato mixture and mix well.
5. Cut the cottage cheese into about 1½" long sticks.
6. Flatten about 1 tablespoon of the potato mixture for each cottage cheese stick. Cover these sticks with the potato mixture and roll into oblong shapes.
7. With damp hands, roll the oblong shapes in the crushed vermicelli.
8. Deep fry till golden brown. Serve hot.

Paneer Kebab Cutlets

Ingredients

1 cup grated cottage cheese
1 cup grated cabbage
½ cup potatoes, boiled and mashed
1 tsp green chilli paste
4 tbsp gram flour
1 tbsp finely chopped coriander leaves
1 onion, finely chopped
2 tbsp oil
Salt to taste

Method

1. Mix the ingredients, except the oil, to form a dough.
2. Divide the mixture into equal-sized balls.
3. Flatten the balls into oval shaped cutlets and keep aside.
4. Heat a non-stick pan. Pour the oil.
5. Fry the cutlets till they are nicely browned on both sides.
6. Serve hot.

Potato Kebab

Ingredients

250 gm small potatoes
1 tsp cumin seeds
1 tsp each of turmeric powder and chilli powder
2 tbsp tomato sauce
1 tbsp lime juice
1 tbsp each of mint leaves and coriander leaves paste
1 tsp chat masala
2 tbsp oil
Oil for deep frying
Salt to taste

Method

1. Boil the potatoes. Peel and prick them with a fork.
2. Apply salt and turmeric powder.
3. Deep fry the potatoes until golden brown.
4. Heat 2 tablespoons of oil and fry the cumin seeds. Add the potatoes and the rest of the ingredients.
5. Saute for a minute and serve hot with a toothpick inserted into each potato.

Paneer Potato Cutlets

Ingredients

100 gm cottage cheese
4-5 green chillies, finely chopped
1 tbsp chopped coriander leaves
4 potatoes, boiled and mashed
1 onion, finely chopped
4 slices of bread
1 cup each of flour and breadcrumbs
1 tsp salt
1 cup finely chopped cabbage or capsicum
A little oil

→

Method

1. Knead the cottage cheese for a minute.
2. Soak the bread in water, then squeeze out the excess water.
3. Mix all the ingredients except the flour, breadcrumbs and oil. Shape the mixture into cutlets.
4. Make a thin paste of the flour with water and a pinch of salt.
5. Dip each cutlet in the paste. Roll it in the breadcrumbs and fry.
6. Serve hot.

Potli Kebab

Ingredients

1 tbsp crumbled cottage cheese
1 cup flour
½ cup boiled and mashed chickpeas
1 tbsp fresh coconut
1 tbsp coriander leaves
2 tbsp butter
1 tsp chilli powder
1 tsp garam masala
Cochineal colour
Oil for deep frying
Salt to taste

Method

1. Mix the flour, 1 tablespoon butter and salt. Knead into a hard dough with warm water.
2. Melt the remaining butter, add the chickpeas, coconut and all the dry *masalas*. Fry for 2 minutes.
3. Remove from the fire and cool.
4. Roll out the dough into small rounds. Then stuff each round with 1 tablespoon of the mixture.
5. Close the dough and shape them into pouches.
6. Draw a line with cochineal colour on the neck of each pouch.
7. Deep fry in the hot oil on a medium flame and serve.

Vegetarian Hariyali Kebab

Ingredients

100 gm spinach
1 tbsp each of mashed cottage cheese and breadcrumbs
1 unripe banana
50 gm corn kernels
1 tsp each of garam masala and chilli powder
½ tsp each of pepper powder and coriander powder
1 tsp green chilli paste
2 tbsp cornflour
1 lime, cut into wedges
1 tsp chat masala
Oil for frying
Salt to taste

Method

1. Wash and boil the spinach with salt in ½ cup water for 5 minutes. Then let it simmer till the water dries up completely. Cool, mash and keep aside.
2. Boil the banana and mash well. Mash the cottage cheese and mix it with the banana.
3. Boil the corn for 10 minutes in 1 cup water, grind and add to the banana mixture.
4. Then add the spinach to the mixture along with the *garam masala*, chilli powder, pepper powder, coriander powder and green chilli paste. Finally add the cornflour and breadcrumbs and mix well.
5. Make round balls and flatten them to a ½" thickness. Fry them in the oil till golden brown.
6. Sprinkle the *chat masala* and serve garnished with the wedges of lime.

PAKORAS, BALLS AND KACHORIS

Cheese Pakoras

Ingredients

100 gm cottage cheese, mashed
50 gm processed cheese, grated
2 slices of bread
3 tsp fresh curd, 4 tsp flour
1 tsp coriander leaves, chopped
3 green chillies, finely chopped
¼ tsp bicarbonate of soda
½ tsp each of chat masala and cumin powder
Oil for deep frying
Salt to taste

Method

1. Soak the bread slices in the curd for 15 minutes.
2. Mash the cottage cheese well and mix it with the soaked bread.
3. Mix in the grated cheese and all the other ingredients.
4. Make small balls and deep fry in the hot oil.
5. Serve hot.

Corn Croquettes

Ingredients

1 cup boiled corn or tinned corn kernels
1 cup mashed cottage cheese
1 tsp each of ginger and garlic paste
¼ cup finely chopped spring onions
½ cup finely chopped onion
1 tsp green chilli paste
1 tbsp each of vinegar, soya sauce and tomato sauce
2 tbsp each of flour and cornflour
½ tsp pepper powder, ¼ tsp ajinomoto
¼ cup breadcrumbs
A pinch of baking powder
Salt and pepper to taste

Method

1. Heat the oil and fry the onion and ginger and garlic pastes till light brown.
2. Add the flour and cornflour and stir-fry for a minute.
3. Add 2 tablespoons water and mix well.
4. Then add the corn, cottage cheese and the rest of the ingredients and mix well.
5. Remove from the fire and cool.
6. Make round balls and then flatten them.
7. Deep fry in the hot oil till golden brown.
8. Serve hot.

Corn Croquettes (pg.57) →

Creamy Paneer Balls

Ingredients

200 gm cottage cheese
100 gm grated processed cheese
½ cup flour
2 tbsp tomato sauce
1 tbsp green chilli paste
1 tsp vinegar
Vermicelli for coating
A little milk or water
Oil for deep frying
Salt to taste

Method

1. Mix the grated cheese and flour till they resemble breadcrumbs.
2. Add the tomato sauce, green chilli paste and vinegar to it. Add salt.
3. Make a batter of the mixture, adding water or milk.
4. Mash the cottage cheese and form into balls.
5. Dip each cottage cheese ball in this batter.
6. Roll the balls in the crushed vermicelli and deep fry untill golden brown.
7. Serve hot.

Paneer Fingers

Ingredients

200 gm cottage cheese, cut into long, thin slices
¼ cup flour
2 tbsp grated cheese
Milk or water
2 tbsp cornflour
2 tbsp tomato sauce
1 tsp lime juice
1 tsp chilli sauce
A pinch of ajinomoto
Salt to taste

Method

1. Mix all the ingredients except the cottage cheese and make a thick batter with the water or milk.
2. Dip each cottage cheese slice in this batter and deep fry until golden brown.
3. Serve hot.

Paneer Kachori

Ingredients

For the kachoris

1 cup flour
2 tbsp butter
½ cup milk
Salt to taste

For the filling

2 tbsp each of crumbled cottage cheese and boiled peas
1 tbsp grated onion
1" piece ginger, 1 tsp oil
½ tsp each of cumin seed powder and garam masala
Oil for deep frying
Salt to taste

Method

1. Mix the butter with the flour till it resembles breadcrumbs.
2. Add salt to taste and mix well.
3. Then add the milk and knead into a soft dough. Cover with a damp cloth and leave for half an hour.
4. For the filling, heat 1 teaspoon oil and saute the onion and ginger in it till the onions turn transparent.
5. Then add the cottage cheese crumbs and peas. Saute for a few minutes.
6. Add all the *masalas* and salt. Mix well and keep aside.
7. Make small balls of the dough. Flatten each ball evenly. Then fill each with about 1 teaspoon of the filling. Close properly to bind the filling in.
8. Heat the oil to a smoking stage. Lower the flame and deep fry the balls till they are golden brown. Serve hot.

Paneer Surprise

Ingredients

200 gm cottage cheese
1½ tbsp lime juice
½ tsp each of ginger and garlic paste
1 tbsp chilli powder
4 tbsp semolina or gram flour
Salt to taste

For the stuffing

1¼ cups fresh corn kernels
¼ cup desiccated coconut
½ cup each of coriander leaves and crushed vermicelli

1 tsp each of garam masala, Kitchen King masala or
curry powder and pomegranate seeds
A pinch of sugar, Oil for deep frying
Salt to taste

Method

1. Mash the cottage cheese. Mix it with the semolina (or gram flour), lime juice, chilli powder, ginger and garlic pastes and salt. Make 8 balls. Flatten these balls. Finely chop the coriander leaves and keep aside.

2. For the stuffing, boil the corn and grind it. Then mix the coconut, coriander leaves, salt, a pinch of sugar and all the *masalas*.

3. Fill this mixture into each flattened cottage cheese base and mould into desired shapes. Roll in the crushed vermicelli and deep fry. Serve hot.

Paneer Pakoras

Ingredients

200 gm cottage cheese
½ tsp each of salt and chilli powder
Oil for deep frying

For the batter

1 cup gram flour
½ tsp each of ginger and green chilli paste
¼ tsp bicarbonate soda, 1 tbsp oil
½ tsp each of turmeric and chilli powder
Water, Salt to taste

→

Method

1. Sieve the gram flour and soda together.
2. Mix all the ingredients for the batter to a thick, creamy consistency. Keep aside for half an hour.
3. Cut the cottage cheese into cubes of desired sizes.
4. Sprinkle salt and chilli powder on them and toss well.
5. Heat the oil to a smoking stage and then lower the flame.
6. Dip the paneer cubes in the batter and coat well. Deep fry on a low flame till golden brown.
7. Serve hot.

Potato Rounds

Ingredients

½ cup cottage cheese crumbs
1 kg potatoes
¼ cup Italino sauce
3 tbsp butter
½ tsp pepper
1 tsp chilli powder
Salt to taste

Method

1. Boil the potatoes, peel and blend them in a blender, with the butter, to a smooth paste.
2. Fill it in an icing bag with a thick nozzle and pipe out whorls on a greased tray. Press the centre of each whorl with a thumb to make a depression.
3. Bake at 200°C till light brown in colour.
4. Make a filling of the cottage cheese crumbs, Italino sauce, pepper, chilli powder and salt. Mix well.
5. Fill the potatoe whorls with this filling and bake again for 5 minutes.
6. Serve hot.

Raj Kachori

Ingredients

1 cup semolina
1 cup flour
1 bottle soda (aerated drink) for kneading
¼ tsp Eno fruit salt (any flavour)
A little salt
Oil for deep frying
Chilli powder to taste

Method

1. Mix all the ingredients except the chilli powder and oil. Knead into a dough using the soda instead of water.
2. Leave aside for half an hour, then roll into *puris*.
3. Sprinkle the red chilli powder over the rolled *puries*, gather from all sides into a pouch, press well and roll out again. Do this with all the other *puris*.
4. Fry on a medium flame till light brown.
5. Serve hot.

Rich Paneer Balls

Ingredients

200 gm cottage cheese
25 gm processed cheese
4 tbsp fine semolina, A pinch of sugar
1 tbsp each of butter and cumin powder
1½ cups breadcrumbs, 1 tsp chilli powder
Oil for deep frying
Salt to taste

For the filling

1 tsp coarsely crushed cashewnuts
6-8 finely chopped raisins

For the batter

2 tbsp flour, 5 tbsp water

Method

1. Mash the cottage cheese well, add the semolina and all the other ingredients. Mix well (except the breadcrumbs and the ingredients for the filling and batter). Divide into 8 portions.
2. Make small balls. Flatten and put a bit of the dry fruit filling in the centre and form into balls. Keep aside.
3. For the batter, mix the flour and water to a smooth, thick consistency.
4. Roll the balls in the flour mixture and then in the breadcrumbs.
5. Deep fry till golden brown. Serve hot.

Spinach Pakoras

Ingredients

1 cup finely chopped spinach leaves
1 onion, finely chopped
½ cup curd
1 tsp green chilli paste
1 tsp chilli powder
200 gm gram flour
½ tsp thymol seeds
Oil for deep frying
Salt to taste

Method

1. Wash the spinach leaves and then finely chop them.
2. Make a thin batter with the rest of the ingredients. Beat well, add the spinach leaves and keep aside for half an hour.
3. Then make small balls of the mixture.
4. Heat the oil in a pan. Deep fry the small balls until they are golden brown.

OTHERS

Crunchy Biscuits

Ingredients

150 gm wholemeal flour
25 gm rice flour
25 gm molasses sugar or castor sugar
100 gm margarine

Method

1. Mix the two kinds of flour and sugar together in a bowl. Rub the margarine into the mixture and knead to form a soft dough.

2. Press into a lightly floured 7" round shortbread mould.

3. Carefully turn out onto a lightly oiled baking sheet and bake at gas mark 3 -160°C - 325°F for 30 - 40 minutes until golden. Cool.

Variations

Shortbread Hearts

1. Roll out the basic mixture and cut into 2" hearts. Bake for 30 minutes. Cool.
2. Break an orange flavoured chocolate bar (150 gm) in a bowl over a pan of simmering water. Stir until it melts.
3. Dip half of each biscuit in the melted orange to coat.

Orange Shortbread

1. Add the grated rind of 1 orange to the basic mixture.
2. Roll out to a ¼" thick rectangle and cut into 2" squares.
3. Mark with the back of a knife to form a pattern. Bake for 30 minutes.

Apricot and Almond Shortbread

1. Spread the basic mixture into a 7½ by 11½" lightly greased Swiss roll tin.
2. Spread low-sugar apricot jam on this, and sprinkle 30 gm nibbed or flaked almonds on it.
3. Bake for 45 minutes. Cut into bars.

Peanut Shortbread

1. Roll out the basic mixture to a 12 by 6" rectangle.
2. Mix together 3 tablespoons honey and 40 gm finely chopped unsalted peanuts.
3. Spread over the shortbread and roll up. Slice at ¼" intervals. Bake for 30 minutes.

Fruit Gazak

Ingredients

15 gm each of almonds, cashewnuts and walnuts
15 gm peanuts
15 gm butter
200 gm sugar
6 green cardamoms, crushed
1 tsp screwpine flavour

Method

1. Mix all the dry nuts and bake in a moderate oven to a golden brown colour to remove the raw flavour.
2. Melt the sugar on a low flame.
3. Add the crushed nuts, butter, crushed cardamoms and screwpine flavour.
4. Stir and remove from the fire.
5. Pour on a greased wooden board and roll out quickly with a rolling pin into 1 cm thickness.
6. Cut immediately into long strips, about 2½ cm long. Let it cool to room temperature and store in an airtight jar.

Barbeque Sauce

Ingredients

½ cup finely chopped onion
4-5 green chillies, chopped
1 each of apple and banana, peeled and chopped
1 tsp salt
½ cup salad oil
2 tbsp sugar
½ cup tomato ketchup
¾ cup vinegar
1 tsp chilli powder
½ tsp pepper
1 tbsp Worcestershire sauce

Method

1. Pour the salad oil in a pan and fry the onion in it till it is golden brown.
2. Add the green chillies and chopped fruits.
3. Stir-fry for 2 minutes, add the vinegar, tomato ketchup, chilli powder, pepper, Worcestershire sauce, sugar and salt. Cook for 5 minutes.
4. Remove from the fire, cool and liquidise in a blender.
5. Serve with any of the barbequed dishes.

Peanut Brittle

Ingredients

350 gm granulated sugar
150 ml water
225 gm golden syrup (readymade)
25 gm butter
350 gm unsalted peanuts, lightly toasted
¼ tsp vanilla flavouring

Method

1. Place the sugar, water and golden syrup in a heavy-based saucepan.
2. Heat gently till the sugar dissolves and then bring to the boil. Boil rapidly until the temperature reaches 150°C.
3. Remove from the fire, add the butter, warm nuts and vanilla. Stir until the butter has melted. Pour into a lightly greased roasting tin and allow the mixture to cool completely.
4. Turn out onto a chopping board and break the peanut brittle into small pieces.

Peanut Brittle (pg.87) →

Roast Potatoes

Ingredients

250 gm small potatoes
1 tbsp dry mango powder
1 tsp pomegranate powder
1 tsp chat masala
1 tsp red chilli powder
2 tbsp ground onion, deep fried
2 tbsp oil
½ tsp each of ginger and garlic paste
¼ cup curd
Salt to taste

Method

1. Parboil the potatoes and peel them.
2. Mix the rest of the ingredients and marinate the potatoes in it for an hour.
3. Arrange them on a skewer and place them in a red hot *tandoor* or barbeque till they are well browned.
4. Serve hot with barbeque sauce or any other dip.

Tandoori Paneer

Ingredients

100 gm cottage cheese
Juice of 1 onion
½ tbsp ginger paste
½ tbsp garlic paste
2 tbsp butter
½ tsp each of cumin powder, chilli powder, garam masala, black salt and white pepper
A pinch of tandoori colour
Salt to taste

Method

1. Mix all the ingredients into a paste except the cottage cheese and butter.
2. Cube the cottage cheese and marinate it in the above paste. Keep aside for 20 minutes.
3. Apply dots of butter on the cubes and bake on a greased tray for 15 minutes.
4. Serve hot.

Cheese Nut Fingers

Ingredients

½ cup cottage cheese crumbs
2 tbsp butter
¼ cup each of flour and grated cheese
$\frac{2}{3}$ cup milk, ½ tsp pepper
1 tbsp celery, finely chopped
3 tbsp cashewnut powder
4 tbsp breadcrumbs
1 tsp green chilli paste
Salt to taste

For the batter

2 tbsp flour, 5 tbsp water
A pinch of salt
Oil for deep frying

Method

1. Heat the butter, add the flour and fry for a minute.
2. Add the milk, cottage cheese crumbs, grated cheese, cashewnut powder, celery, pepper, green chilli paste and salt. Mix well.
3. Spread the mixture on a greased plate and freeze it.
4. Remove from the refrigerator and cut into fingers.
5. Then mix the ingredients for the batter.
6. Roll the fingers in the flour batter and then in the breadcrumbs.
7. Deep fry in hot oil until golden brown. Serve hot.

Mathri

Ingredients

250 gm flour
1 level tsp salt
6 tbsp water
3½ tsp melted ghee
½ tsp caraway seeds
Ghee for deep frying

Method

1. Sift the flour and put all the ingredients together in a bowl.
2. Rub the mixture till it resembles breadcrumbs and then knead with water. Make 18 to 20 round balls. Roll into very thin rounds.
3. Fold into a triangle-shaped *mathri*. Press the pointed side with the rolling pin (but be careful not to press the layers).
4. Deep fry in the ghee on a medium flame. Turn it frequently until brown.
5. Drain on a wire rack. Serve hot or store in air-tight jars when cool.

Crunchy Greens

Ingredients

450 gm spring greens
¼ tsp salt
2 tsp castor sugar
25 gm soft brown sugar
Oil for deep frying

Method

1. Wash the greens and remove the tough stalks. Using absorbent kitchen paper, dry the greens thoroughly.
2. Place about 6 leaves on top of each other and roll up tightly. Shred very finely. Dry again.
3. Heat the oil in a deep frying pan. Fry a few greens at a time for about 30 seconds, or until the bubbles subside.
4. Remove when crisp, drain on absorbent kitchen paper. Fry the remaining greens.
5. Add salt and castor sugar, mix well.
6. Place in a serving dish, sprinkle over the soft brown sugar. Serve hot or keep warm in an oven, covered with foil.

Paneer Manchurian

Ingredients

200 gm cottage cheese, cut into 1" cubes
Oil for deep frying

For the batter

¼ cup each of cornflour and flour
¼ tsp baking powder
Water
Salt and pepper to taste

For the sauce

1 tbsp each of garlic and green chilli paste
4 tbsp oil
1 tsp cornflour
½ cup water (for the cornflour)
½ cup finely chopped spring onions
2 tbsp each of soya sauce and vinegar
¼ tsp ajinomoto
Salt to taste

Method

1. Make the batter by mixing all the ingredients to a smooth consistency.
2. Dip the cottage cheese cubes in the batter and deep fry till light brown in colour. Keep aside.
3. For the sauce, heat 4 tablespoons of oil, fry the garlic and green chilli pastes.
4. Add the soya sauce, vinegar, ajinomoto and salt. Then add the cornflour dissolved in water. Continue stirring till the sauce thickens.
5. Add the fried cottage cheese cubes at the time of serving. Garnish with the chopped spring onions and serve hot.

Paneer Masala Vada

Ingredients

200 gm cottage cheese, grated
100 gm Bengal gram
2 cups milk
1 tsp ginger paste
1 tbsp green chilli paste
1 tbsp finely chopped coriander leaves
1 tsp garam masala
1 tbsp each of cumin powder, chilli powder and coriander powder
Oil for frying, A few curry leaves
Salt to taste

Method

1. Boil the Bengal gram in the milk on a medium flame until tender, or until the milk dries up completely. Cool and grind in a grinder.
2. Add the grated cottage cheese to it along with all the *masalas* and salt (if the mixture is too dry, add a little milk to it).
3. Shape into flat rounds. Deep fry or shallow fry. Serve hot with coconut chutney.

Spicy Paneer Crispies

Ingredients

200 gm cottage cheese
1 grated onion
½ tsp each of ginger and garlic paste
½ cup breadcrumbs
½ cup coriander leaves
2 tbsp flour
2 tbsp oil
½ tsp chilli powder
1 tsp Kitchen King masala
Oil for deep frying
Salt and pepper to taste

For the filling

1 tbsp cream
½ tbsp butter
1 tsp grated cheese
2 tsp green chilli paste
½ tsp each of finely chopped cashewnuts and raisins

Method

1. Mix the ingredients for the filling and freeze.
2. Pour 2 tablespoons oil in a frying pan. Fry the onion and ginger and garlic pastes. Add the flour and cook for 2 minutes.
3. Add the *masalas*, coriander leaves and breadcrumbs. Remove from the fire and cool.
4. Fill this mixture with the frozen filling and make into oblong-shaped rolls or into any other desired shape. Deep fry until golden brown. Serve hot.

Shredded Wheat Flap Jacks

Ingredients

100 gm each of butter and castor sugar
1 tbsp syrup, 50 gm rolled oats
3 shredded wheat biscuits, crushed
A pinch of nutmeg

Method

1. Pour the syrup with the butter and sugar in a pan. Heat till the butter melts. Stir in the remaining ingredients until well mixed.
2. Press into a greased 20 cm square cake tin and bake at 180°C, gas mark 4 for 25 minutes or until golden.
3. Remove from the oven and mark into rectangles with a sharp knife. Leave to cool before removing from the tin.

Nutty Cluster Cups

Ingredients

50 gm mixed nuts
100 gm plain chocolate bar

Method

1. Roughly chop the nuts.
2. Break the chocolate into pieces and place in a saucepan. Cook for 3 minutes on full flame, or till the chocolate melts.
3. Stir in the nuts and mix lightly until just coated with the chocolate.
4. Drop tablespoonfuls of nuts onto a non-stick baking paper and leave to set. The top layer should appear smooth.

Vegetable Parcels

Ingredients

2 tbsp vegetable oil
1 onion, finely chopped
1 red or green chilli, seeded and chopped
1" piece ginger, peeled and grated
2 tsp curry powder
1 tsp ground cumin
½ tsp ground turmeric
1 tbsp plain flour
450 gm vegetables (carrots, potatoes etc.), peeled and diced
200 ml vegetable stock
50 gm each of peas and sweetcorn kernels
Oil for brushing and deep frying

For the dough

300 gm flour
A pinch of salt
1 tbsp oil
A little lukewarm water
1 tsp thymol

Method

1. Mix all the ingredients for the dough. Knead to a firm dough and keep aside for 20 minutes.

2. Heat the vegetable oil in a saucepan and fry the onion, chilli and ginger for 5 minutes, or until soft.

3. Stir in the curry powder, cumin, turmeric and flour and fry gently for 1 minute.

4. Add the diced vegetables to the pan and stir in the stock. Bring to the boil, then lower the flame and simmer covered for 20 minutes.
5. Add the peas and sweetcorn kernels and then continue simmering until most of the liquid has been absorbed.
6. Divide the dough into 8 portions and make balls. Then flatten them out to form small rounds. Place a tablespoon of the filling on one end of a flattened round. Fold over the end at a diagonal to form a triangle. Continue folding up, making a triangle shaped parcel of the filling.
7. Repeat the process with the remaining filling and dough.
8. Heat the oil for deep frying. Fry 2 or 3 parcels at a time for 3 to 4 minutes until golden. Drain the parcels on kitchen paper and serve hot.

Strawberry Cake

Ingredients

½ tin condensed milk
½ cup milk
¼ tsp bicarbonate of soda
¼ tsp salt
¼ tsp yellow colour
1 cup flour, sifted
1 tsp baking powder
5 tsp butter
1 tsp strawberry essence

Method

1. Melt the butter over a low flame and remove from the fire. Then beat the butter, milk, condensed milk, colour and essence together.
2. Add the sifted flour, salt, bicarbonate of soda and baking powder to this and mix thoroughly in one direction.
3. Line a cake tin, 10 cm in diameter with greased brown paper.
4. Pour the mixture in it and bake in a moderate oven (350°F).
5. Cool and serve.

Spinach and Lentil Layer

Ingredients

50 gm onion
1 small garlic clove
50 gm red lentil, ¼ tsp ground ginger
A pinch each of ground chilli powder and cumin powder
2 tsp tomato puree
1 tsp sesame seeds
Salt and ground black pepper to taste
Oil for greasing

For the spinach layer

250 gm roughly chopped spinach
1½ tbsp cornflour

Method

1. Peel the onion and garlic. Then finely chop the onion and crush the garlic. Place in a small pan with the lentil, ginger, chilli powder, cumin powder, salt, pepper and tomato puree. Add 300 ml cold water.
2. Slowly bring the mixture to the boil, half covered and simmer for 30 minutes until the liquid has completely evaporated and the lentil is tender.
3. Steam the spinach in boiling water till tender. Season with salt and pepper. Drain thoroughly.
4. Mix the cornflour with the spinach and mash well till it forms a thick paste.
5. Grease a shallow square tin. Spoon the spinach paste into the tin and spread evenly.
6. Bake for 5 minutes until just firm to the touch.

Spinach and Lentil Layer (pg.117) →

For assembling

1. Cut the spinach square in half, then cut each piece into three.
2. Spread the lentil paste on each piece. Pile up to form two stacks.
3. Roast Fry the sesame seeds in a small non-stick pan until golden. Scatter over the spinach stack.
4. Serve immediately with carrot and shredded cabbage salad.